HOW THEY INTERPRET THE BAPTISM OF THE HOLY GHOST

Dr. John H. Manigo

ISBN: 979-8-218-42316-2

Library of Congress Control Number:
2024919608

Printed in the USA

Authored by
Dr. John H. Manigo

Editor
Kingdom Builders Publications
Lakisha S. Forrester

Cover Design
Dreamstime Image
LoMar Designs

Photographer
Louise James

DEDICATION

To the ones reading this, God loves you and desires that you dwell eternally in Heaven with Him.

To the memory of my deceased Beloved, Evangelist Patricia Lynne Clark Manigo, May 8, 2017. She was loved by all whom she encountered. Her colleagues said she was special.

CONTENTS

DEDICATION III

CONTENTS IV

ACKNOWLEDGMENTS 7

PREFACE 9

INTRODUCTION 11

MY TESTIMONY 12

AN INSPIRING MOMENT 15

TO FEEL IS BY FAITH IN CHRIST JESUS.......... 19

A TYPE OF THE HOLY SPIRIT 22

WHAT MUST WE DO TO BE SAVED?................... 24

SCRIPTURES ON SALVATION 25

THIS IS JESUS! 26

HAVE YOU SEEN JESUS? 28

TO THOSE WHO FORGET GOD 31

HELL IS... 32

CONTENDING FOR OUR FAITH 35

FROM SAUL TO APOSTLE PAUL 37

THE HOLY GHOST 39

PENTECOST 42

SPEAKING IN TONGUES....................................... 46

UNDERSTANDING THE CLEAR DOCTRINE OF MARK 16:16............................. 49

RECONCILE THAT THE ORIGINAL DISCIPLES DID NOT UNDERSTAND WHAT JESUS MEANT 54

THE CONCLUSION AND REAL TRUTH OF THE MATTER.................................... 59

WATER BAPTISM 60

BAPTIZED IN WHOSE NAME? 62

BAPTISM OF THE HOLY GHOST 63

MINIMIZING CONFUSION 65

MAKE A JOYFUL NOISE 68

LOVE 69

SLEEP NOT 72

SLEEPING ON THE PROMISES 78

1 PETER 5:8 80

THE GOOD SHEPHERD VS. THE THIEF 81

WIN THEM TO CHRIST 85

WAKE UP CALL 86

THE HOLY GHOST 88

BLASPHEMY: THE UNFORGIVEABLE SIN 90

ARE YOU SERIOUS? 92

MY PRAYER FOR YOU 95

THE VOICE OF STRANGERS 96

ONCE SAVED, ALWAYS SAVED 99

SANCTIFICATION 102

THE ASCENDED 103

WHAT SAY YE? 107

REPENTANCE 109

PEACE BE UNTO YOU 112

NO OTHER GOD 114

SPIRITUAL NOURISHMENT 119

THE THREE R'S 120

THE BIBLE IS... 122

READING THE WORD 123

AN INTERPRETATION OF CHRIST 125

AT THE REVELATION OF JESUS CHRIST 132

ABOUT THE AUTHOR 138

ACKNOWLEDGMENTS

My beloved wife, Evangelist Patricia Lynne Clark Manigo and I moved from Conway, South Carolina to Columbia, South Carolina in 1987. She was hired to work at Columbia International University as a clerk in the accounting department. We lived in a mobile home not too far from her job.

One day, a white, Christian woman invited us to her church's revival. We agreed to go. From the outside, I thought it was just a Southern Baptist Church. Before we entered, I told my wife that I could hear noise. I was surprised, but excited. When we got inside, the church looked like Pentecost. There was such a great move of the Holy Ghost.

We went on to visit other churches—some Baptist and some African Methodist Episcopal. Thankfully, they all had one thing in common...Pentecost was in action!

"For God is not the author of confusion, but of peace, as in all churches of the saints," according to **1 Corinthians 14:33**. Whether a church is deemed as a white church, black church or any other ethnicity, that doesn't matter. The most important quality churches should exhibit is the leading of the Holy Ghost. When that occurs, Pentecost can break out anytime, at any location, and in any denomination.

PREFACE

I look to a day when people will not be judged by the color of their skin, but by the content of their character.
--Martin Luther King, Jr.

Years ago, I used to say if the world was filled with only one skin color, then it would be boring. Although there is so much focus on skin color and ethnicity in the present-day world, neither of those facets will get us into heaven. **Ecclesiastes 12:7** says, "Then shall the dust return to the earth as it was: and the spirit shall return unto God who gave it," and the "Lord will judge his people" (**Psalm 135:14**).

It is important for us to remember that our skin color won't change, but it is imperative that our hearts do. In order for that to happen, we must accept Jesus Christ as our personal Lord and Savior and allow (not block) the Holy Spirit from residing in our hearts, minds, and souls.

For we are his workmanship, created
in Christ Jesus unto good works,
which God hath before ordained that
we should walk in them.

Ephesians 2:10

INTRODUCTION

I was born with normal hearing. At three-weeks old, I developed meningitis and lost my hearing as a result.

When I express myself, I do so through the senses or in a poetic nature, using descriptive words. My goal in writing this book is to help those who don't know Christ, or those who do and have found themselves in a backslidden state. It's not too late. Hear the unadulterated truth of the Word and come to the Lord or back to the Lord. Repent and flee from idolatry, and from any thought, idea, or deed that's preventing you from living in the fullness of God.

Then Jesus answering said unto them, Go your way, and tell John what things ye have seen and heard; how that the blind see, the lame walk, the lepers are cleansed, the deaf hear, the dead are raised, to the poor the gospel is preached. And blessed is he, whosoever shall not be offended in me.

Luke 7:22-23

MY TESTIMONY

And Moses said unto the Lord, O my Lord, I am not eloquent, neither heretofore, nor since thou hast spoken unto thy servant: but I am slow of speech, and of a slow tongue. And the Lord said unto him, Who hath made man's mouth? Or who maketh the dumb, or deaf, or the seeing, or the blind? Have not I the Lord? Now therefore go, and I will be with thy mouth, and teach thee what thou shalt say.

Exodus 4:10-12

Isn't this the perfect "no excuses are accepted" scripture ever written? I understand how Moses felt. Many lack confidence because they listen to and believe what the world has deemed as imperfections. They take that unproductive chatter as truth and use it as an excuse not to push ahead or strive for more. We must remember that we were created in His image—fearfully and wonderfully made, in fact (**Genesis 1:27**; **Psalm 139:14**). Therefore, we have all power in our hands because it comes from Him. God promised to be there every step of the way, so we must trust Him. If He called us to it, He would get us through it. "Let the weak say, I'm strong" (**Joel 3:10**). His "grace is sufficient for you, for my power is made perfect in weakness" (**2 Corinthians 12:9**).

With power and authority given to us by the Lord Jesus Christ and through His strength, let us commit to the Lord wholeheartedly, by doing His Will and going wherever He leads us.

Exodus 4:10-12 became a living testimony for me at the age of 20 during a one-week revival. In February 1972, at South

Carolina School for the Deaf and the Blind, I preached the Gospel of Jesus Christ to the poor, needy, strangers, the hearing, and the deaf. It was such a powerful move of God. On that day, I was able to sing using both my voice and sign language.

I have learned that even in nervousness, there is security—a certain confidence, astute resolution—when you know the Lord has sent you to deliver a message and speak a word of edification, encouragement, and truth. He will guide you every step of the way if you are in His will and following obediently.

I can do all things through Christ
which strengtheneth me.

Philippians 4:13

AN INSPIRING MOMENT

Patricia and I met Reverend Doctor Andrew Foster in my hometown, Conway, SC, at a Christian Fellowship Church. At the time we accepted the invitation to sing there, we had no idea he would be the featured guest. When a friend told us, we were truly excited. Dr. Foster was a role model in the deaf community.

He was called the Father of Deaf Education in Africa with notable achievements. He helped young, deaf Africans and African Americans—fostering the vision of bringing light, knowledge, and hope, allowing them a chance to see beyond their circumstances. He committed to these efforts full-time, thus starting many Christian Mission Schools for the deaf in Africa, including co-founding the African Bible College for the Deaf with his wife.

I can go on and on about this great man. In addition to being an advocate for the deaf, he committed to the call of Christ on his life. Being deaf didn't stop his destiny, and he wanted to make sure it wasn't going to stop anyone else's either.

After my wife and I met him, he was killed three years later in a tragic airplane crash into a mountain in Rwanda.

I will never forget when he asked me if I could speak and sign at the same time. I responded, "Yes." He told me he couldn't.

That's what I believe our lives should be about. Bringing hope to the hopeless, joy to the joyless, loved to the unloved, and knowledge to the unlearned. Our life should be a testimony of compassion towards our brothers and sisters.

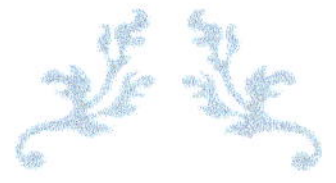

What? know ye not that your body is
the temple of the Holy Ghost which is
in you, which ye have of God, and ye
are not your own? For ye are bought
with a price: therefore glorify God in
your body, and in your spirit, which
are God's.

1 Corinthians 6:19-20

TO FEEL IS BY FAITH IN CHRIST JESUS

Acts 17:27-28 states, *"That they should seek the Lord, if haply they might **feel** after him, and find him, though he be not far from every one of us: For in him we live, and move, and have our being; as certain also of your poets have said, For we are also his offspring."* It is truly awesome being an offspring of a loving, graceful, and merciful Father.

John 3:8 states, *"The wind bloweth where it listeth, and you hear the sound of it, but cannot tell where it comes from and where it goes. So is everyone who is born of the Spirit"* (NKJV). That scripture is the perfect explanation to give to those who say God doesn't exist because He is unseen by the naked eye. He's an invisible God, they say. But, I submit to you that He is very much visible and "a very present help in trouble" (**Psalm 46:1**).

Like the wind, we see the effects of the Father. We feel the wind, we see the rustling of the leaves in the trees, the toppled over trash cans in the street, and often the heavy, blustering gusts during tornadoes and hurricanes. Likewise, we feel the Spirit of God; we see the workings of the Father throughout our lives.

The wind exists because God exists. The wind blows because God has blown life into His creation. Oh yes, God is real. Absolutely. Undeniably. Unequivocally. He's ready to blow a fresh wind of clarity into our lives and into our very beings if we just accept Him as Lord and Savior. Let Him order our footsteps. Let Him do a great work in us. Let He, the Chief Surgeon, perform a masterful work. Let Him create in us a clean heart (**Psalm 51:10**). Let Him gut out the addictions, habits, and wrong thinking (our sinful nature) so that we may represent Him to the fullest. Let Him turn darkness into light within our lives. **Matthew 5:16** says, "Let your light so shine before men, that they may see your good works, and glorify your Father which is in heaven."

We can **feel** Jesus, the Risen Savior, by believing in Him through faith. In **Mark 11:22**, Jesus told us to, "Have faith In God" and that the "just shall live by faith" (**Habakkuk 2:4, Romans 1:17, Galatians 3:11**).

SCRIPTURES ON FAITH

Hebrews 11:1

Hebrews 11:6

Matthew 15:28

Matthew 17:20

Ephesians 2:8

Romans 10:8-11

Romans 1:17

Romans 5:1-2

Mark 11:22-24

2 Corinthians 5:7

A TYPE OF THE HOLY SPIRIT

A spider man is a type of Christ.
A spider is a type of the Holy Spirit.
A spider web is a type of the Holy Spirit.

A tool spinning thread box is a type of Christ.
A thread is a type of the Holy Spirit.

A rope knot is a type of Christ.
A rope is a type of the Holy Spirit.

A belt buckle is a type of Christ.
A belt is a type of the Holy Spirit.

A hand is a type of Christ.
Fingers or fingernails, thumb or thumbnails are a type of the
Holy Spirit.
A foot or feet is a type of Christ.
Toenails are a type of the Holy Spirit.
The whole body is a type of God.
Two arms like wings are a type of the Holy Spirit.

A soap bar is a type of Christ.
Soap bubbles are a type of the Holy Spirit.
A blowing bubble stick is a type of Christ.
Blowing bubbles is a type of the Holy Spirit.

The earth is a type of God.
The raining showers are a type of the Holy Spirit.
A rainbow is a type of the promise of the Holy Spirit.

Snowing as white is a type of the Holy Spirit.
A footprint is a type of the Holy Spirit.
A cotton flower is a type of the Holy Spirit.
Once blown, it will fly away or spread to various places to
reach, touch, feel, or smell.

WHAT MUST WE DO TO BE SAVED?

So then faith cometh by hearing, and hearing by the word of
God.
Romans 10:17

Seek the Lord.
Feel after Christ.
He is not far.
He is near us.
He is among us.
He is with us.
The Word is near thee.
Open your mouth.
Confess with your mouth.
God raised Jesus from the dead.
Believe in your heart.
Believe unto righteousness.
Repent of your sins.
Ask for forgiveness.
Open your eyes.
See the salvation of the Lord.
Thou art saved,
By grace,
Through faith,
In Jesus Christ.

SCRIPTURES ON SALVATION

Acts 4:12

Titus 3:5

John 3:16-18

Acts 16:31

Romans 10:9-10

Philippians 2:12-13

Romans 1:16

Titus 2:11-14

1 Thessalonians 5:9

Psalm 37:39

THIS IS JESUS!

Jesus
Christ
Holy King
Prophet
Lord
Risen Savior
Messiah
Redeemer
The Lamb of God
Son of God
Son of Man
Good Shepherd
High Priest
King of Israel
King of the Jews
Prince of Peace
Author and Finisher of our Faith
Bright and Morning Star
Emmanuel
Light of the World
Comforter
Deliverer
Burden Bearer
Rock
Sword and Shield
Wheel in the Middle of a Wheel
Refuge
King of Kings
Lord of Lords
Counselor
Wonderful
Matchless
Friend

Beloved Son
Mediator
Intercessor
True Vine
Branch
Lion of Judah
I Am
The Way, the Truth, and the Life
The Sweetest Name
Bread of Life
Head Lifter
Chief Cornerstone
Living Word
Bridegroom
The Same Yesterday
Today
Forever

HAVE YOU SEEN JESUS?

Jesus has shown us the Father.
The Father and Jesus are One.
Jesus is in the Father.
The Father is in Jesus.
Therefore,
The Father is near us.
The Father walks among us.
The Father is with us.
He is in our spirit,
Heart,
Soul,
Body.
Knock and the door shall open.
He won't leave or forsake us.
He is waiting for us all.
He's coming back again.
Every knee shall bow.
Every tongue shall confess.
Jesus is Lord.

Howbeit when he, the Spirit of truth,
is come, he will guide you into all
truth: for he shall not speak of
himself; but whatsoever he shall hear,
that shall he speak: and he will shew
you things to come.

John 16:13

And if it seem evil unto you to serve
the Lord, choose you this day whom
ye will serve; whether the gods which
your fathers served that were on the
other side of the flood, or the gods of
the Amorites, in whose land ye dwell:
but as for me and my house, we will
serve the Lord.

Joshua 24:15

TO THOSE WHO FORGET GOD

You will be aware of and sense you are in Hell.
You will see, smell, breathe, hear, feel, and be in hell.
Your body, hands, and feet will burn.
You will feel pain, hurt, and extreme heat.
You will scream, holler, and yell for help.
There will be no relief.
Your fate will be sealed in eternity.

HELL IS...

Woe to the preachers who say there is no hell. Woe to any of you who neglect the truth of the Word. Every blood bought believer knows that Hell is real. Plus, the Bible says it is so. Below are necessary descriptors to remind us of the seriousness and importance of repenting and changing our wicked ways so that we don't end up in that dreadful place for eternity.

Eternal damnation
Sheol
Bottomless pit
Hades
The grave
The payment for the penalty of sin
Fire and brimstone
Burning wind
Fiery oven
Flames of fire
Judgment by fire
An unquenchable fire
The furnace of fire
Casted into
Darkness
The lake of fire
The smoke of torment
The weeping and gnashing of teeth
Lost souls
Refused to accept Christ
Unrepented
Tormented and tortured by demons

Brutality
Day and night
The abyss
God's wrath upon the disobedient

For we wrestle not against flesh and blood, but against principalities, against powers, against the rulers of the darkness of this world, against spiritual wickedness in high places.

Ephesians 6:12

CONTENDING FOR OUR FAITH

Behold, He comes quickly.
The reward is in His hand.
The imminent return of Christ;
The second coming of Christ.
Be prepared to meet the Lord thy God.
Be sober.
Armor up:
Helmet of Salvation,
Breastplate of Righteousness,
Belt of Truth,
Shoes of the Gospel of Peace,
Shield of Faith.
Take up your Sword.
Abide in
Hope,
Faith,
Love.
Pray for your salvation.
Pray to be clothed in righteousness.
Pray that you be found worthy,
Pray for salvation of the lost ones.
Intercede on their behaves.
Spread the gospel.
He that wins souls is wise.

Whatever you do, work at it with all
your heart, as working for the Lord,
not for human masters.

Colossians 3:23

FROM SAUL TO APOSTLE PAUL

Apostle Paul's story was one of the most intriguing. He was a man who happily persecuted Christians as Saul. He had an encounter with Jesus on Damascus Road. He was knocked off his beast, incurred a name change, and herein lies Apostle Paul, one of the most prolific, on fire people in the Bible. He was hungry for God and was not ashamed. He proclaimed the Gospel everywhere he went. Whether he was free or bound, he didn't stray from the truth. He was willing to die for his belief.

Would you be willing to walk away from everything and everyone that doesn't fit in God's plan for your life? "While we look not at the things which are seen, but at the things which are not seen: for the things which are seen are temporal; but the things which are not seen are eternal" (**2 Corinthians 4:18**). Be not attached to things of the world. Because in a vapor, they will all vanish. Only what you do for Christ will last.

SCRIPTURES ON BELIEF

John 14:1

Acts 16:31

John 6:29

Mark 1:15

Luke 8:50

Mark 11:24

1 Thessalonians 4:14

Philippians 1:29

1 John 4:1

John 11:40

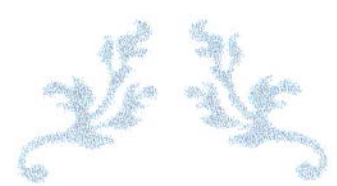

Then Peter said unto them, Repent,
and be baptized every one of you in
the name of Jesus Christ for the
remission of sins, and ye shall receive
the gift of the Holy Ghost.

Acts 2:38

THE HOLY GHOST

John 14:26

When people say they've received the Holy Ghost, what do they actually mean?

One group says they "caught" the Holy Ghost, referencing they are dancing uncontrollably in the spirit. Another group is saying they have accepted Jesus Christ as their personal savior and the Holy Ghost has come to reside in them—to comfort, advocate, and help them through the good and difficult seasons of their lives. The third group is referring to speaking in tongues.

So, what's the right answer? Well, you can't catch the Holy Ghost. He's not thrown in the air like a baseball or basketball. In fact, we invite Him to live inside us when we receive salvation. The Holy Ghost can cause an overwhelming sense of emotions, whereas some cry, some dance, etc. The Holy Ghost is a gift—a gift that is given to us to cleanse us from sin and all unrighteousness.

Many people dance in church and say it's the Holy Ghost. Not all of them are believers, so can that be so? Absolutely not! Not every saved person dances or runs around the church. So, does that mean they don't have the Holy Ghost? Again, that answer is no. Dancing is not a requirement, but living a submitted life is. Praise and worship should be a part of honoring God, but that may look different from everyone.

We know there are many attention seekers in church who are operating with another spirit. It may look like God, but it isn't. It may dance like, speak in tongues like, pray like, teach like, but isn't God. They are imitators, being led by an unclean spirit. When the music stops, their so-called praise and worship stops on cue.

Make no mistake, **Galatians 6:7** says, "Be not deceived; God is not mocked: for whatsoever a man soweth, that shall he also reap."

PENTECOST

And when the day of Pentecost was fully come, they were all
with one accord in one place.
Acts 2:1

Apostle Peter was the main speaker on the Day of Pentecost.
Pentecost is the first revival in the history of humanity. It was
a powerful experience—one that was carried by the Holy
Spirit. It occurred after Jesus was crucified, resurrected, and
ascended to Heaven. There were about one hundred and
twenty disciples in the upper room, in prayer on one accord.
"And suddenly there came a sound from heaven as of a
rushing mighty wind, and it filled all the house where they
were sitting. And there appeared unto them cloven tongues
like as of fire, and it sat upon each of them. And they were all
filled with the Holy Ghost, and began to speak with other
tongues, as the Spirit gave them utterance" (**Acts 2:2-4**). The
language spoken in the Holy Ghost was understood by all
people—in their native languages.

I believe this experience was so powerful because of the
spirit of agreement. **Matthew 18:19** says, "That if two of you
shall agree on earth as touching any thing that they shall ask,
it shall be done for them of my Father which is in heaven."

It reminds of the Tower of Babel story in the Bible. Initially,
everyone spoke the same language. They too were on one
accord as they devised a plan to build "a city and a tower,
whose top may reach unto heaven" and make a name for
themselves" (**Genesis 11:4**). The Lord confounded their
language as a result. He was not going to allow them to carry
out that plan because "nothing will be restrained from them,
which they have imagined to do" (**Genesis 11:6**).

Can you imagine that? Man becoming so wise in their eyes, that they had enough entitlement to believe they had a right or access to Heaven—the Holy Place—at their whim. That's the same type of entitled spirit when James and John (the sons of Zebedee) requested that Jesus grant them permission to "sit, one on thy right hand, and the other on thy left hand, in thy glory" (**Mark 10:37**). *"But to sit on my right hand and on my left hand is not mine to give; but it shall be given to them for whom it is prepared,"* Jesus stated in **Mark 10:40**.

One thing I know for sure is, God can make a believer out of the skeptics. He can make what seems impossible to be possible, like He did in **Acts 2:8**: "And how hear we every man in our own tongue, wherein we were born?" That was truly remarkable at Pentecost, and could only have been done with the Holy Ghost.

Just know: The power of agreement can be used for good (Pentecost) or for selfish reasons (Babel). The desire to be God is what got Lucifer kicked out of heaven (**Isaiah 14:12–21**).

Man must recognize that there is only one God. The desire to make a name for oneself is usually what leads those who never served or once served the Lord into other religions, practices, and beliefs that are not of God—ones that are rooted in paganism, idolatry, and new age mysticism. They put all their money (literally) on being one with the world, participating in yoga practices, crystals, tarot cards, crystal balls, etc. They open themselves up to these competing spirits and find themselves in major confusion and are even tortured by the demons, thus having to get fully delivered and make their way either back to Christ or to Christ for the very first time.

Likewise the Spirit also helpeth our infirmities: for we know not what we should pray for as we ought: but the Spirit itself maketh intercession for us with groanings which cannot be uttered.

Romans 8:26

SPEAKING IN TONGUES

And these signs shall follow them that believe; In my name shall they cast out devils; they shall speak with new tongues.
Mark 16:17

1 Corinthians 14:23 states, "If therefore the whole church be come together into one place, and all speak with tongues, and there come in those that are unlearned, or unbelievers, will they not say that ye are mad?" Many, unfortunately, have described speaking in tongues as unintelligible prattle, gibberish, babblings of fanaticism, and meaningless jargon.

I think many people fear tongues because they don't understand what it is or the purpose. Quite honestly, it has been made to be a spooky thing, often the source of jokes and imitations in the entertainment industry or in normal, everyday conversations. You may have people "speaking in tongues" on demand and even practicing how to do it.

We are to "discern between the righteous and the wicked, between him that serveth God and him that serveth him not" (**Malachi 3:18**). That can be a difficult task if you have not spent time with the Lord. We have to humble ourselves in the sight of the Lord, admit that we don't know everything, that we sometimes miss it, and that we are not always able to distinguish light from dark because we may not be as mature as we pretend we are.

There is hope for us if we are willing to put our relationship with the Lord at the center of our lives and seek Him with all diligence. Our Father is available day and night because He doesn't sleep or slumber. We can go to Him, and He will give us the answer through whatever method He chooses. We have to pay attention, learn His voice, learn His ways, and learn Him in general.

So, beware of what looks like or sounds like tongues, because it may actually not be so. A person may have an unclean spirit operating in them, using a false tongue. The Lord said, in **1 John 4:1**, "Beloved, believe not every spirit, but try the spirits whether they are of God: because many false prophets are gone out into the world." This is where we get the phrase, "Test the spirit by the spirit."

When it comes to speaking in tongues in general, it is important to understand that it is a gift. Through salvation and the Holy Ghost, God has put certain gifts inside of us. Not everyone will have the same gift. That's why it's important not to be boastful. When one think they are more anointed because they can speak in tongues, and that God loves them more, they are heading into a dangerous, prideful territory.

In fact, Apostle Paul was the perfect example of not letting the gift of tongues cause him not to walk in humility. He stated in **1 Corinthians 14:18-19**, "I thank my God, I speak with tongues more than ye all: yet in the church I had rather speak five words with my understanding, that by my voice I might teach others also, than ten thousand words in an unknown language."

It is easy for one to become out of order in church. Like anywhere else, there are protocols, and the Bible is clear on speaking in tongues and the order of such. **1 Corinthians 14:40** states, "Let all things be done decently and in order." "If any man speak in an unknown tongue, let it be by two, or at the most by three, and that by course; and let one interpret. But if there be no interpreter, let him keep silence in the church; and let him speak to himself, and to God" (**1 Corinthians 14:27-30**).

Life is not a competition. We will experience many bumps and triumphs along the way. "The race is not to the swift, nor the battle to the strong, neither yet bread to the wise, nor yet riches to men of understanding, nor yet favour to men of skill; but time and chance happeneth to them all" (**Ecclesiastes 9:11**).

Speaking in tongues won't get you to Heaven and it certainly won't keep you out of Hell. Our obedience (or lack thereof) will determine our fate at the end of this world.

UNDERSTANDING THE CLEAR DOCTRINE OF MARK 16:16

Just in case there is a confusion about the doctrine of Mark 16:16, let's discover the clear message of this text.

He that believeth and is baptized shall be saved; but he that believeth not shall be damned.
Mark 16:16

First of all, let us consider who is talking. When we see the words in red, it means Jesus is talking. To whom he is talking? He is teaching the disciples on salvation.

We will call this portion, the A and B Plan.

Plan A means if a sinner believes the gospel and is baptized he would now repent (Godly sorrow) then he has received salvation (saved).

Plan B is the opposite of believing, repenting, and receiving salvation (being saved). Jesus was making this very plain. You have two options, believe, repent, and be saved or do not believe, do not repent, do not be baptized, and be damned.

You have your own will; therefore you are placed with the decision whether to live according to the salvation plan or not.

Jesus sent the disciples out to teach this important life lesson.

Of course, the disciples did not understand what Jesus was talking about. In fact, Jesus wasn't understood most times by the disciples or many other people who heard his teachings.

John, the Baptist used his own personal words seven times; I indeed baptize with water, and He (Jesus) baptize with the

Holy Spirit. **Matthew 3:11, Mark 1:8, Luke 3:16** and **John 1:26-27, 33 Acts 13:24-25, Acts 1:4-5, Acts 11:16, Acts 13:24-25**

Jesus used the word once to *"remind"* His original disciples that John *"truly"* baptize with water, but ye shall be baptized with the Holy Spirit not many days hence. **Acts 1:4-5**

Peter *"reminded"* himself to tell the original disciples and others that he *"remembered"* the word of the Lord, how that he said, "John indeed baptized with water; *"but"* ye shall be baptized with the Holy Spirit." **Acts 11:16**

Paul found certain disciples and he asked and said, "Have ye received the Holy Spirit since ye believed?" **Acts 19:2** Paul also remembered hearing John: **Acts 13:24, 25**.

Jesus told the original disciples to wait for the promise of the Father. **Luke 24:49, John 14:16**. Jesus' disciples "did not know" what the promise of the Father was going to do concerning "another Comforter." **John 14:26**

John did not even know what Jesus might do, but John knew *"only"* that Jesus sent John to baptize with water. John *"only knew"* that Jesus would baptize with the Holy Ghost. At that time, John did not know, understand or realize what Jesus would do to baptize with the Holy Ghost because of the Holy Ghost (nothing was given about when it would happen). **John 7:37-39, John 20:17. Acts 8:16, Acts 13:24-25**

So John baptized *"only"* with water baptism for repentance. Jesus was baptized in water by John the Baptist for a good reason. John did not understand *"why"* Jesus need to be baptized in water, but Jesus was baptized in water to show us His example to follow **Matthew 28:19-20**. Jesus also showed His example of His death burial and resurrection. **Romans 6:3-4, Acts 8:16, Acts 19:2-4, Galatians 3:27, 1st Peter 2:21**

Peter and John and the rest of the disciples did not know what Jesus was talking about when He said in **Acts 1:4,** Wait for the promise of the Father. They heard correctly. But what did it mean when this statement was uttered, *ye shall be baptized with the Holy Ghost not many days hence Only Jesus knew.* **Acts 1:5**. Jesus also says in **Luke 24:49**, "…*I send the promise of my Father upon you: "but" tarry until ye be ended with power from high."* Only Jesus knew the answer. Only Jesus knew the detail.

Jesus was saying some things! "*Be endued with power from on high.* **Luke 24:49** "*Ye shall receive power after that the Holy Ghost is come upon you: and ye shall be witnesses unto me"*… **Acts 1:8ª**. *"Receive ye the Holy Ghost."* **John 20:22**.

The followers of Jesus had to hang in there with Him. He had their curiosities heightened. When they thought they had a handle on a few of the things he was saying, then here came more riddles and conundrums that followed.

Words such as these before his death, *I am the Bread of life; In three days, I will rise again; I am the Resurrection of Life;* so is the Coming of the Son of Man be; coming in the cloud with great glory; and speaking with new tongues. **Mark 16:17.**

The disciples of Jesus had been trained for three years with Jesus by His side. Jesus did not give all that was needed to be done, but Jesus did promise this, *"But the Comforter, which is the Holy Spirit, whom the Father will send in my name, He (the Comforter, the Holy Spirit) will teach you all things, and bring all things to "your remembrance," whatsoever I have said unto you.* **John 14:26-31, John 15:26-27**

Jesus gave His original disciples His finally and farewell statement before He was taken up to glory. He said, "But ye shall receive power after that the Holy Spirit is come upon you: and ye shall be witnesses unto me both in Jerusalem, and in Judaea and in Samaria, and unto the uttermost part of the earth." **Acts 1:8**. He also told them about speaking with new tongues. **Mark 16:17**

Jesus continued teaching and preaching, although He knew the disciples and the other followers were completely clueless. But the revelation of what He spoke of was slowly being revealed. Here are some Bible conversational proofs.

And while Jesus had spoken those things, while they beheld (looked), He was taken up; and a cloud received Him out of their sight. **Acts 1:9**

The disciples heard Jesus' finally and farewell statement: "You shall receive power after the Holy Spirit come upon you. You shall be witnesses for Jesus. They did not understand what was Jesus saying and what Jesus meant. They were instructed to go to the upper room for prayer and the 120 names gathering. Check it out in **Acts 1:13-15**, **Acts 2:2.**

And there appeared unto them cloven tongues like as of fire, and the fire rested upon each one of the 120 gatherings. Acts 2:3

Again the original disciples and the rests of the gatherings still did not know, still did not understand, still did not get the idea of what Jesus "meant:" But this strange thing; this strange evident; this strange doctrine was getting close! (on the way!!!) Only Jesus knew the intent and purpose for it all.

The original disciples of Jesus and the rest of the gatherings were filled with the Holy Ghost!!! Not only the Holy Ghost; and they began, to speak with other tongues (languages) as the Spirit gave them utterance. Acts 2:4, Mark 16:17

Everything was new to the followers and now are beginning to have a sense of understanding *"after"* three years in the ministry with Jesus.

One of the disciples was Apostle Peter, preached a mighty Pentecostal message under the Holy Spirit power. The people, the strangers, the pilgrim, from a strange land; sojourners in the land, were glad to receive the powerful word of God; the Word of Jesus Christ. The result was 3,000 souls were saved that day, on the Pentecostal event in the city of Jerusalem. **Acts 2:41**

And fear came upon every soul; and many wonders and signs were done by the apostles (the original of disciples of Jesus). **Acts 2:43**

And they continued steadfastly in the apostles' doctrine (the teaching that Jesus taught them for three years in the ministry) and fellowship and in breaking of bread, and in prayers. **Acts 2:42**

RECONCILE THAT THE ORIGINAL DISCIPLES DID NOT UNDERSTAND WHAT JESUS MEANT

The word *meant* is of course the past tense of *mean* and is defined as intent, purposed to do, or a mind to do. Whatever a person intends, his purpose would be.

Here is what happen in the Bible as we read and study carefully:

Jesus used the word once to *remind* His disciples that John *truly* baptized with water, but ye shall be baptized with the Holy Spirit not many days from here now on. Acts 1:4-5

Peter reminded himself to tell the original disciples and others that he remembered the word of the Lord, how he said, "John indeed baptized with water; but ye shall be baptized with the Holy Spirit." Acts 11:16

Paul found certain disciples and asked them, "Have ye received the Holy Spirit since ye believed?" Acts 19:2. Paul also remembered hearing John: Acts 13:24, 25

No one *knew* or *understood* what Jesus meant when He said, For John, truly baptized with water; but ye shall be baptized with the Holy Ghost not many days hence. Acts 1:5. Jesus *knew* from Joel 2:28, 29. Jesus told the original disciples to wait for the promise of the Father. Luke 24:49, John 14:16. Jesus' disciples did not know what the promise of the Father was going to do. Jesus was speaking of *another Comforter*. John 14:16, 26, John 15:26, 27

John didn't know what Jesus would do, but he knew Jesus sent him to baptize with water. John only knew that Jesus would baptize His children with the Holy Ghost. At that time John didn't understand or realize how Jesus would baptize with the Holy Ghost because the Holy Ghost was not yet given; because He was not yet glorified. John 7:37-39, John 20:17. Acts 8:16, Acts 13:24-25.

John baptized *only* with water baptism unto repentance. His whole sermon was to believe on Jesus. (Acts 19:4) John baptized Jesus in water for a good reason, however he didn't understand *why* Jesus needed to be baptized in water. Matthew 3:13-15, 16-17

Jesus also showed His example of His death burial and resurrection. Romans 6:3-4, Acts 8:16, Acts 19:2-4, Galatians 3:27. This was the water baptism John the Baptist did to his cousin, the Lord Jesus Christ. Matthew 3:11-15, Mark 1:8, Luke 3:16, John 1:33, Acts 1:5, Acts 11:16, 1st Peter 2:21

Peter, John, and the rest of the disciples didn't comprehend when He said in Acts 1:4 *wait for the promise of the Father…* They heard right, but had no clue of its meaning. As to, when the message, *"I send to you the promise of my Father upon you: but tarry until ye be endued with power from high."*

Jesus did say: *"Be endued with power from on high"* Luke 24:49, *"Shall receive power after that the Holy Ghost is come upon you: and ye shall be witnessed unto me"* Acts 1:8, and *"Receive ye the Holy Ghost."* in John 20:22.

Jesus breathed on them, and they received the Holy Ghost. They were still, they were quiet; *and* they were blessed to receive, by knowing that Jesus was alive and that made the disciples glad when they saw the Lord. John 20:20

Jesus appeared to the certain disciples and said, *"Peace be unto you."* Luke 24:36. Then Jesus said, *"Behold my hands and my feet, that it is I myself; handle me, and see; for a spirit (or a soul) hath not flesh and bones, as ye see me have."* Then Jesus asked the disciples, *"Have ye here any meat!"* (food) Luke 24:39-41, 42-44

Jesus reminded His original disciples the many important teachings that Christ was to gather; to rise from the dead; and that repentance and remission of sins should be preached in His name among all nations, beginning at Jerusalem, and to witness of these things which they had seen and had been taught for three years. Jesus repeatedly said to His original disciples: "*And behold, I send the promise of my Father upon you: "but" tarry (stay, wait) ye in the city of Jerusalem until ye be endued with power from on high.* Luke 24:49

Jesus opened His original disciples' understanding so they might comprehend the scriptures. Luke 24:45-49

The disciples heard Jesus use these few words such as *His death; I am the Bread of life; In three days, I will rise again; I am the Resurrection of Life; so is the Coming of the Son of Man be; coming in the cloud with great glory; and speaking with new tongues.* Mark 16:17

The disciples had been trained for three years by Jesus; however Jesus did not give all that was needed to be understood Jesus did promise this. "*But the Comforter, which is the Holy Spirit, whom the Father will send in my name, He (the Comforter, the Holy Spirit) will teach you all things, and bring all things to "your remembrance," whatsoever I have said unto you.* John 14:26-31, John 15:26-27

Jesus gave the disciples His farewell statement before He was taken up to glory. He said, "*But ye shall receive power after that the Holy Spirit is come upon you: and ye shall be witnesses unto me both in Jerusalem, and in Judaea and in Samaria, and unto the uttermost parts of the earth.* He also told them about speaking with new tongues. Mark 16:17, Acts 1:8. While Jesus had spoken those things, while they beheld (looked), He was taken up; and a cloud received Him out of their sight. Acts 1:9

And when the day of Pentecost was fully come, they were all

with one accord in one place. Acts 2:1

They did not know what to expect, except to sit where they were to rest. Then suddenly they heard the coming of a sound from heaven as of a rushing mighty wind and the rushing mighty wind filled all those who were gathered. Acts 2:2

And there appeared unto them cloven tongues like as of fire, and the fire rested upon each of them. Acts 2:3

While the disciples was in the midst of a lesson by the Lord, they were sent to the upper room to be endued with power, they experienced a strange thing. This strange evidence; this strange doctrine was getting close to their knowing! It was on the way! Only Jesus knew the purpose; only Jesus knew the intention and the details.

The disciples and the rest of the gatherers were filled with the Holy Ghost! Not only were they filled with the Holy Ghost, but they began to speak with other tongues (languages) as the Spirit gave them utterance. Acts 2:4, Mark 16:17

The disciples and the rest did not know the result was to be filled with the Holy Spirit and to speak with other tongues as the Spirit gave them utterance. Only Jesus knew the plan; the purpose; the intent and all. Everything was new to them. They understood *after* three years in the ministry with Jesus. Mark 16:17

One of the disciples was Apostle Peter. He preached a mighty Pentecostal message under the Holy Spirit power. All the people were glad to receive the powerful word of God; the Word of Jesus Christ. The result was 3,000 souls were saved that day, on the Pentecostal event in the city of Jerusalem. Acts 2:41

And fear came upon every soul; and many wonders and signs were done by the apostles. Acts 2:43

And they continued steadfastly in the apostles' doctrine (the teaching that Jesus taught them for three years in the ministry) fellowship, breaking of bread, and in prayers. Acts 2:42

And all that believed were together, and had all things common; sold possessions and goods parted (divided or share) them to all men as every man had need. Acts 2:44-45

And they, continuing *daily* with one accord in the temple, and breaking bread from house to house, did eat their meat (food) with gladness and singleness of heart. Acts 2:46

Praising God, and having favor with "all the people." And the Lord (Himself) added to the church "daily" such as should be saved (requirement for salvation; repentance, taught by God the Father). Many others came, but the Lord knew who were saved and who were not saved. John 6:65, 71, Acts 15:8-9, 11, 18, II Timothy 2:19, Romans 8:16-17

Finally, the original disciples understood *afterwards*! Not before in the presence of Christ's ministry for three years they had been taught. However, Jesus did mention speaking with new tongues in Mark 16:17.

The Spirit is still at work today until Jesus comes "the second time." Revelation 22:7, 12, 20. Hebrews 9:28.

Did John ever say: "I indeed baptize you with the Holy Spirit? No! John knew that Jesus was to baptize with the Holy Spirit. John did baptize in the wilderness and did preach the baptism of repentance for the remission (forgiveness or pardon) of sins, but John the Baptist did not baptize with the Holy Spirit. Just Water Baptism. Mark 1:4, Matthew 3:11.

THE CONCLUSION AND REAL TRUTH OF THE MATTER

Finally, after seeing the marvelous workings and teachings of Jesus, the original disciples understood. They could now teach it because they in part believed it. There was still much to put together about Jesus, the Spirit of God, Baptism with water, and Baptism with the Holy Ghost.

The Holy Ghost is a two-fold work for the Christ follower. The Holy Ghost within, and the Holy Ghost upon. The Holy Ghose within is for Holiness and Sanctification and the Holy Ghost upon is for the power to do ministry (as on the day of Pentecost).

Jesus knew what the speaking with new tongues meant or what was to be. Jesus mentioned speaking with new tongues. *And they were filled with the Holy Spirit and began to speak with other tongues as the Spirit gave them utterance; in order to spread the good news of Jesus Christ to the world that they might be saved.* **John 20:30-31**

 And the Spirit is still at work today and will be until Jesus' return "the second time." **Revelation 22:7, 12, 20, Hebrews 9:28**.

WATER BAPTISM

Jesus answered, *Verily, verily, I say unto thee, Except a man be born of water and of the Spirit, he cannot enter into the kingdom of God.*

John 3:5

John baptized Jesus in **Matthew 3:13-17**, although he didn't feel qualified because of who Jesus was (and still is). He felt Jesus should baptize him instead because he was the Chosen One. What John failed to realize is that he too was chosen, from the foundations of the earth to do what he was assigned to do. Besides, obedience is better than sacrifice (**1 Samuel 15:22**), and John did what was commanded of him.

"And Jesus, when he was baptized, went up straightway out of the water: and, lo, the heavens were opened unto him, and he saw the Spirit of God descending like a dove, and lighting upon him: And lo a voice from heaven, saying, *This is my beloved Son, in whom I am well pleased*" (**Matthew 3:16-17**). Oh a glorious day that was!

Many say that water baptism isn't important. The fact that Jesus was baptized and many more were baptized by water in the Bible makes it important. Water baptism is a spiritual and symbolic act—a cleansing, an outward declaration that we believe in the Lord Jesus Christ and are now in union with Him. "When we are lowered into the water, it is like the burial of Jesus; when we are raised up out of the water, it is like the resurrection of Jesus" (**Romans 6:4, MSG**).

What is the word water baptism or baptize?

Water baptism is a picture to show that we are baptized in water to Christ's death, Christ's burial and Christ's resurrection: after we believe in Jesus Christ as our Lord and Savior in our heart by faith. Romans 6:3-4

Baptize means to dip unto, to go under water, to plunge into. We believe the way Jesus taught us how to be baptized when John the Baptist baptized Jesus in the Jordan River in order for Jesus "to fulfill" all righteousness. Matthew 3:15 and Matthew 28:19-20

Types of Water Baptism:

- Matthew 3:15-17

- Matthew 28:18-20

- Jesus' Death – Romans 6:3, 4

- Jesus' Burial – Romans 6:4

- Jesus' Resurrection – Romans 6:4

Conclusion:

If we understand the distinction and definition between Water Baptism and the Spirit Baptism, we won't be entangled in erroneous teachings and doctrines.

BAPTIZED IN WHOSE NAME?

Teaching them to observe all things whatsoever I have commanded you: and, lo, I am with you always, even unto the end of the world. Amen.
Matthew 28:20

In the modern-day church, once the naysayers finally realized that water baptism is important, another religious argument came about regarding whose name to baptize the people in. "Do we baptize them in Jesus's name?" or "Do we baptize them in the name of the Father, Son, and of the Holy Ghost?"

Because of the confusion and preachers being sensitive to some who will say it doesn't count if you do it this way or that way, to settle the chatter, some just say, "I baptize you in Jesus Christ. I baptize you in the name of the Father, Son, and the Holy Ghost."

BAPTISM OF THE HOLY GHOST

John was sent as a witness to tell the people about the coming of the Preferred One—the Messiah, in which he stated, "whose shoe's latchet I am not worthy to unloose" (**John 1:27**). *When John saw Jesus, he said, "Behold the Lamb of God, which taketh away the sin of the world"* (**John 1:29**). *"And I knew him not: but that he should be made manifest to Israel, therefore am I come baptizing with water* (**John 1:31**).

Jesus said, in **Acts 1:5**, *"For John truly baptized with water; but ye shall be baptized with the Holy Ghost not many days hence."*

How do we get baptized in the Holy Ghost? Peter told us in **Acts 2:38**, *"Repent, and be baptized every one of you in the name of Jesus Christ for the remission of sins, and ye shall receive the gift of the Holy Ghost."*

This scripture shows us that we cannot receive the Holy Ghost until we have confessed our sins, asked for forgiveness (repented), and accepted the salvation of the Lord, and the indwelling of the Holy Ghost. Salvation indicates that we believe that Jesus Christ is the Son of God, that He died for our sins, and was resurrected in three days. To be clear, The Holy Ghost does not dwell in unbelievers; those who have not accepted Christ through salvation.

Prior to **Acts 2:38**, it wouldn't be possible to baptize anyone in the name of the Father, Son, and the Holy Ghost because the Holy Ghost had not come yet. Jesus was still on earth and hadn't ascended back to Heaven.

Once Jesus fulfilled that mandate on His Life (the death and resurrection), the power from on high and the Holy Ghost was now activated, and it was released upon the people at Pentecost. Released means the power of; the indwelling of the spirit.

MINIMIZING CONFUSION

God has already told us He is not the author of confusion (**1 Corinthians 14:33**) and that we should come to him when we need wisdom (**James 1:5**).

I believe we can get rid of a lot of confusion, unnecessary arguments, or twisting of scriptures within the church, if we keep **Deuteronomy 4:2** in the back of our minds. It states, "Ye shall not add unto the word which I command you, neither shall ye diminish ought from it, that ye may keep the commandments of the LORD your God which I command you." Simply put, "Don't add to or take away from the Word of God." **Revelation 22: 18-19**

Saying you don't know is probably better than to make up something. Remember, *"We are of God: he that knoweth God heareth us; he that is not of God heareth not us. Hereby we know the spirit of truth, and the spirit of error"* (**1 John 4:6**).

SCRIPTURES ON BAPTISM

Ephesians 4:5

Galatians 3:27

1 Corinthians 12:13

Romans 6:3-5

Colossians 2:12

Matthew 28:19

But he answered and said, It is written, Man shall not live by bread alone, but by every word that proceedeth out of the mouth of God.

Matthew 4:4

MAKE A JOYFUL NOISE

Let the heavens rejoice, and let the earth be glad; let the sea roar, and the fulness thereof. Let the field be joyful, and all that is therein: then shall all the trees of the wood rejoice.
Psalm 96:11-12

Make a joyful noise unto the Lord, all ye lands.
Serve the Lord with gladness: come before his presence with singing.
Know ye that the Lord he is God: it is he that hath made us, and not we ourselves; we are his people, and the sheep of his pasture.
Enter into his gates with thanksgiving, and into his courts with praise: be thankful unto him, and bless his name.
For the Lord is good; his mercy is everlasting; and his truth endureth to all generations.
Psalm 100:1-5

LOVE

John 3:16: *For God so loved the world, that he gave his only begotten Son, that whosoever believeth in him should not perish, but have everlasting life.*

1 THESSALONIANS 4:13-18

But I would not have you to be ignorant, brethren, concerning them which are asleep, that ye sorrow not, even as others which have no hope.
For if we believe that Jesus died and rose again, even so them also which sleep in Jesus will God bring with him.
For this we say unto you by the word of the Lord, that we which are alive and remain unto the coming of the Lord shall not prevent them which are asleep.
For the Lord himself shall descend from heaven with a shout, with the voice of the archangel, and with the trump of God: and the dead in Christ shall rise first:
Then we which are alive and remain shall be caught up together with them in the clouds, to meet the Lord in the air: and so shall we ever be with the Lord.
Wherefore comfort one another with these words.

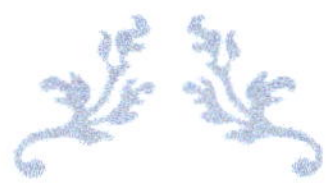

When thou liest down, thou shalt not
be afraid: Yea, thou shalt lie down,
and thy sleep shall be sweet. Be not
afraid of sudden fear, Neither of the
desolation of the wicked, when it
cometh. For the Lord shall be thy
confidence, And shall keep thy foot
from being taken.

Proverbs 3:24-26

SLEEP NOT

Watch and pray, that ye enter not into temptation: the spirit indeed is willing, but the flesh is weak.
Matthew 26:41

In **Revelation 16:15**, the Lord says, *"Behold, I come as a thief. Blessed is he that watcheth, and keepeth his garments, lest he walk naked, and they see his shame."*

This scripture serves as a reminder that we must closely pay attention to what is going on in us and around us. In order to do so, we must be watchful (awake).

Staying awake isn't necessarily in the physical sense, but spiritually. However, there are times when God needs you to physically get up in the wee hours of the morning or late at night to sup with him. He might have a word to share, a revelation, a prophetic word to release, an answer to your question, a solution for your problem(s), or direction for your life. When the spirit that is within you awakens you, no matter what time it is, discipline it to rise when God says rise, and sleep when God says sleep. I know it can be hard, but we have to train and discipline our flesh, bringing it under subjection, to follow the voice of the Lord. The main point is, we have to be cognizant that the Lord is watching and expects us to be obedient and vigilant unto Him.

Another example of sleep, in the natural and spiritual sense was found in **Matthew 26:40-45**. Jesus knew what was going to happen to Him, and so did the disciples. He prepared them for the day that was going to come that He would be beaten, mocked, and ridiculed unto death. (Yet, he would rise again. Hallelujah!) Can you imagine the physical pain He knew He was going to endure? *He fell on his face, and prayed, saying, O my Father, if it be possible, let this cup pass from me: nevertheless not as I will, but as thou wilt* (**Matthew 26:39**).

I am sure the disciples were sorrowful and felt helpless, knowing what the Savior was going to endure for us all on the way to the Cross. Jesus asked them to stay awake and pray, but they did not do so. I wonder how He felt knowing that in the time of His most critical need, the people He poured into, nourished and cared for, didn't bring subjection unto their flesh, and stay awake to pray like he asked. Jesus was carrying a huge burden—giving His life for all of us.

For those who think it wasn't natural for Jesus to have a bit of misgivings about this whole thing, that's really unfair. Yes, Jesus knew that suffering was to come in that great manner. Yes, if there was a chance that the same result could happen without Him being beat mercifully than dying, I'm sure He would have liked to opted to do so (as many of us would have wanted also in the flesh). However, that wasn't what the Father wanted, and so it had to be as it was written. Jesus understood that. Think about it, could we handle even one stripe of that caliber to our body as Jesus endured many more than that?

Isaiah 53:5 says, "But he was wounded for our transgressions, he was bruised for our iniquities: the chastisement of our peace was upon him; and with his stripes we are healed."

We are to suffer with Christ. I know it gets hard, especially when it seems we've had nothing but suffering days. I promise you it will all be worth it in the end, as we glory with Him forevermore. Remember, God said He will never leave us or forsake us (**Hebrews 13:5**). We like to say and sing about what the enemy means for evil, God will turn it for good (**Genesis 50:20**), but we need to believe it in our heart.

We've addressed the watchful part of **Revelation 16:15**. The next part of the scripture instructs us to keep our garments. This is a symbolization of us being clothed in righteousness as children of God. **Ephesians 5:27** says, "That he might present it to himself a glorious church, not having spot, or wrinkle, or any such thing; but that it should be holy and without blemish."

Who is the church God is referring to? Is it a building? No, church is the people. The people who He calls His. The ones who accepts, worships, praises, and follows Him.

How do we rid ourselves of the spots, wrinkles, and blemishes? Well, it is definitely not on our own strength, power, or knowledge. It's impossible to do so. It takes the power of the Holy Ghost and a made-up mind on our part. God wants to purge us with hyssop, wash us, and clean us up so that we will be "purer than snow" and "whiter than milk" (**Lamentations 4:7**).

In **Psalm 51:10**, David cried out, "Create in me a clean heart, O God; and renew a right spirit within me." God wants us to be vessels of honor and sanctification; presenting us back to Himself, preparing us for a good work (**2 Timothy 2:21**).

The last part of **Revelation 16:15** addresses the nakedness and shame. For some, it has taken public humiliation (like the woman caught in adultery) in **John 8** for them to stop and turn from their wicked ways. When some our caught, they immediately blame God for not protecting them from the embarrassment. **Numbers 32:23** tells us that our sin will find us out. Not everything we do, or every sin we commit is exposed on public platforms for the world to see. Those private sins, the ones no one knows about, but God, are just as important for us to get rid of. We can only do so if we are willing. I pray that God strips us of disobedience and our sinful nature.

God corrects us because He loves us. Mature believers in Christ shouldn't feel exposure is a bad thing (privately or publically) especially since the Lord most definitely has sent several warnings, either through them personally by the Holy Spirit, others, the Word, a message, etc. We know God loves us (even in exposure; correction). We should be grateful that He has given us another chance and are alive to get it right. We cannot live with hypocrisy and without repentance. Well, we can, but we won't be at peace.

When it comes to the things of God, how many of us put them off, saying we will get to it tomorrow? "It" can be salvation, morality and ethics, reading the Bible, prayer, worship, obedience, sacrifice, purpose, an instruction, etc. Our personal narratives can't come before God's. We are spiritual beings in a physical body. We are His spiritual houses.

If Jesus came back right now, where will He find the condition of your house? Will your house be in order? Will it be slept clean, through prayer, repentance, and obedience? Or, will he find spots and sprinkles of sin and filth in the corners and crevices of your heart? Will he find "bitterness, and wrath, and anger, and clamour, and evil speaking"— all forms of malice, that He's instructed us to put away (**Ephesians 4:31**)?

Are you a spiritual procrastinator? Do you feel that you have so much time, that you can afford to wait? We don't know the exact number of hair on our head (**Luke 12:7**) or our life expectancy, but God does. Do we really want to risk it?

Let Him wash you. Once you've repented of your sins, changed your thinking, then go on about the work of the Lord. Don't look back like Lot's wife (**Genesis 19:26**) or continue to harp over the things you've done. The Lord has forgiven you because you asked, and didn't ask amiss. You asked in sincerity, desiring to do His will—making Him Lord and ruler over your life; surrendering it all to you. Forgive yourself and forget "those things which are behind, and reaching forth unto those things which are before" (**Philippians 3:13**). "For as the heaven is high above the earth, so great is his mercy toward them that fear him. As far as the east is from the west, so far hath he removed our transgressions from us" (**Psalm 103:11-12)**. Remember, "There is therefore now no condemnation to them which are in Christ Jesus, who walk not after the flesh, but after the Spirit" (**Romans 8:1**).

HEBREWS 12:6-11

For whom the Lord loveth he chasteneth, and scourgeth every son whom he receiveth.
If ye endure chastening, God dealeth with you as with sons; for what son is he whom the father chasteneth not?
But if ye be without chastisement, whereof all are partakers, then are ye bastards, and not sons.
Furthermore we have had fathers of our flesh which corrected us, and we gave them reverence: shall we not much rather be in subjection unto the Father of spirits, and live?
For they verily for a few days chastened us after their own pleasure; but he for our profit, that we might be partakers of his holiness.
Now no chastening for the present seemeth to be joyous, but grievous: nevertheless afterward it yieldeth the peaceable fruit of righteousness unto them which are exercised thereby.

SLEEPING ON THE PROMISES

Behold, he that keepeth Israel shall neither slumber nor sleep. The Lord is thy keeper: The Lord is thy shade upon thy right hand. The sun shall not smite thee by day, nor the moon by night. The Lord shall preserve thee from all evil: He shall preserve thy soul.
Psalm 121:4-8

How much sleep have you lost due to worry and not trusting God?

Rest, my dear readers. Rest in His Word. Rest in who He is. "He is a rewarder of them that diligently seek him" (**Hebrews 11:6**). I promise you; God is worth it!

Always remember, "The Lord shall fight for you, and ye shall hold your peace" (**Exodus 14:14**). Therefore, "Be careful for nothing; but in every thing by prayer and supplication with thanksgiving let your requests be made known unto God. And the peace of God, which passeth all understanding, shall keep your hearts and minds through Christ Jesus" (**Philippians 4:6-7**).

Ye also, as lively stones, are built up a
spiritual house, an holy priesthood, to
offer up special spiritual sacrifices,
acceptable to God by Jesus Christ.

1 Peter 2:5

BE WATCHFUL AND VIGILANT

Amos 4:12

Revelation 3:11

Revelation 22:7

Revelation 16:15

Revelation 22:12

Genesis 1:31

Genesis 3:22

Genesis 15:4

Proverbs 19:12

1 PETER 5:8

THE GOOD SHEPHERD VS. THE THIEF

And Jesus answered and said unto them, Are ye come out, as against a thief, with swords and with staves to take me? (**Mark 14:48**)

Verily, verily, I say unto you, He that entereth not by the door into the sheepfold, but climbeth up some other way, the same is a thief and a robber (**John 10:1**).

Be sober, be vigilant; because your adversary the devil, as a roaring lion, walketh about, seeking whom he may devour (**1 Peter 5:8**).

The thief cometh not, but for to steal, and to kill, and to destroy: I am come that they might have life, and that they might have it more abundantly (**John 10:10**).

As the thief is ashamed when he is found, so is the house of Israel ashamed; they, their kings, their princes, and their priests, and their prophets (**Jeremiah 2:26**).

I am the good shepherd: the good shepherd giveth his life for the sheep (**John 10:11**).

Whom resist steadfast in the faith,
knowing that the same afflictions are
accomplished in your brethren that
are in the world. But the God of all
grace, who hath called us unto his
eternal glory by Christ Jesus, after that
ye have suffered a while, make you
perfect, stablish, strengthen, settle
you. To him be glory and dominion
for ever and ever. Amen.

1 Peter 5:9-11

HEAVEN AND ETERNITY

Luke 23:42-43

Revelation 21:1-4

Matthew 5:10

John 14:2-4

Matthew 6:19-21

2 Corinthians 5:1-8

Revelation 21:22-27

Genesis 1:1

Philippians 3:20-21

John 3:16

Revelation 22:1-5

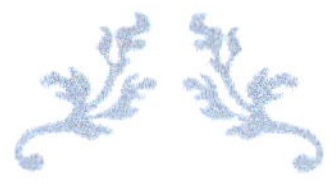

But he answered and said, It is written, Man shall not live by bread alone, but by every word that proceedeth out of the mouth of God.

Matthew 4:4

WIN THEM TO CHRIST

How is it then, brethren? When ye come together, every one of you hath a psalm, hath a doctrine, hath a tongue, hath a revelation, hath an interpretation.
1 Corinthians 14:26

A Psalm
(Spiritual hymn)

A Doctrine
(Teaching; a set of beliefs)

A Tongue
(Language)

Revelation
(To speak; word of knowledge; prophecy)

Interpretation
(Explanation of tongue; scripture)

Edify
(To encourage; build up; exhort)

WAKE UP CALL

He which testifieth these things saith, Surely I come quickly.
Amen. Even so, come, Lord Jesus.
Revelation 22:20

Jesus is coming soon
Are you ready for Him?
Prepare now
Be ready
Get ready
Repent
Ask for forgiveness
Be baptized
Receive the gift of the Holy Spirit
When the saints go marching in,
Will you be in the number?

And whosoever shall speak a word
against the Son of man, it shall be
forgiven him: but unto him that
blasphemeth against the Holy Ghost it
shall not be forgiven.

Luke 12:10

THE HOLY GHOST

The Spirit of the Lord
Source of power
Helper
Sent to teach all things
Witnesses in Jerusalem
In all of Judea
And Samaria
And to the end of the earth

SCRIPTURES ON THE HOLY GHOST

Matthew 3:11

John 3:5

John 14:26

John 15:26

Acts 2:1-5

BLASPHEMY: THE UNFORGIVEABLE SIN

Disassociating
No allegiance to the Holy One
Hardened heart
Not receptive to truth
The truth is Christ
Denial of visible evidence
Of the Deity
Rejecting the Truth
The Message
The Instruction
The Power
What say ye disciple or unbeliever?
Rejecting the spirit
Conscious decision to reject
The Comforter
The Holy Ghost
Injurious talk
Utterances of blasphemies
Speaking words of contempt, disrespect, and folly
Unworthy act
Lack of reverence
Blinded by sin
No guilt
No Conviction
Clearly knowing better
Willfully rejecting
The divine.
The guide
The comforter

The restrainer
Without God, Jesus, and the Holy Ghost,
Spiritual death will be the fate
Lost into eternal darkness
No escape
No forgiveness will be granted
Unworthy act against God
Rebellious
Prideful
Refuse to Submit

ARE YOU SERIOUS?

Just like no man knows the day or hour that the Lord will return (**Matthew 24:36**). Although doctors tell you how much time you have left to live when you have a serious illness based on their scientific opinions, they are not God. God knows how long we will live and the number of every hair on our head. We always think we have more time, often putting off things until tomorrow with the assumption that we control our own destiny, fate, or even life span.

In reality, some even consciously put off being saved. "Oh, I will get saved this Sunday." Then, years, months, weeks, and days will pass by. Some, unfortunately, find themselves in the position of having no choice left when they are on their deathbeds seeking the Lord.

When they say they aren't ready to be saved, what do they mean? Some are normally referring to not being ready to give up their idolatrous or sinful ways. They know that living for Christ will mean they have to put off the flesh, operate in the spirit, cut some things, people, and ways loose; surrendering completely unto God. They know they have to live for Christ and may have to go off on a path of the unknown, one that may be less comfortable because they have to agree to trust God completely and let Him lead. They know they have to surrender unto Him, meaning His ways and His plans for their lives. Many aren't ready to give up that control. So let's keep praying that they get ready (that we all do) before it's too late.

Jesus was very specific in the instructions given to Him by the Father. **John 6:37-38** says, *"All that the Father giveth me shall come to me; and him that cometh to me I will in no wise cast out. For I came down from heaven, not to do mine own will, but the will of him that sent me."*

BLESSED ARE THE POOR IN SPIRIT

1 Thessalonians 1:6

Matthew 5:3

1 Peter 1:8

Luke 6:23

Psalm 89:15-18

Luke 8:15

Jude 1:20

John 16:20

Philippians 4:1

James 1:4-8

James 4:10

John 16:23

John 17:3

MY PRAYER FOR YOU

1 Peter 1:8

Whom having not seen, ye love; in whom, though now ye see him not, yet believing, ye rejoice with joy unspeakable and full of glory.

1 John 1:4

And these things write we unto you, that your joy may be full.

Matthew 25:21

His lord said unto him, Well done thou good and faithful servant: thou hast been faithful over a few things, I will make thee ruler over many things: enter thou into the joy of thy lord.

Luke 6:23

Rejoice ye in that day, and leap for joy: for, behold, your reward is great in heaven: for in the like manner did their fathers unto the prophets.

THE VOICE OF STRANGERS

It is important to know the Word of God (Bible) for yourself so that you can debunk doctrinal errors and heretical teachings. Being able to discern and separate what man says versus what God says concerning holiness, salvation, and His expectations will allow us to keep ourselves on the right path—which is the one God paved for us.

In order to combat the wiles of the devil and keep our minds free to hear and obey the Lord, we must carve out time to spend with God, seeking Him in the Word and in the spirit, as well as praise, exhort, and worship Him.

To keep the devil at bay and to keep oppressive and depressive thoughts from overtaking us, particularly looking at the state of the world now, I would garner to say we should seek God daily, hour-by-hour, minute-by-minute, and second-by-second—keeping Him always in our thoughts. Remember, we are in a war. The devil wants our soul, but it belongs to God. Contend with that enemy and fight! Fight in the spirit, war for the breakthrough of your mind, your family, and for generational curses to cease to exist.

Philippians 4:8 says, *"Finally, brethren, whatsoever things are true, whatsoever things are honest, whatsoever things are just, whatsoever things are pure, whatsoever things are lovely, whatsoever things are of good report; if there be any virtue, and if there be any praise, think on these things."* Hallelujah!

When we are newly saved creatures, we are considered to be babes in Christ. We generally start out on fire for God, wanting to learn as much as possible and sharing our testimony with whoever will listen. Often (but certainly not for all), we can have the propensity to not know the Word as well, be confused by scriptures, and the Lord has to handle us with care because we may be fragile. So many of us start off drinking milk because we are not yet able to handle the unadulterated meat of the word as **1 Corinthians 3:2** suggests. But that's not where any of us should want to stay. There is no room for complacency as blood bought believers. We shouldn't strive to remain the same, doing just enough to get by. According to Hebrews **5:13-14**, *"For every one that useth milk is unskilful in the word of righteousness: for he is a babe. But strong meat belongeth to them that are of full age, even those who by reason of use have their senses exercised to discern both good and evil."*

So, how do we do that? **2 Timothy 2:5** tells us to, *"Study to shew thyself approved unto God, a workman that needed not to be ashamed, rightly dividing the word of truth."*

We are blessed beyond measure to have the Holy Spirit. He clarifies things, corrects us, helps us to interpret scripture, and shows us how to apply the Word to our lives. If we let Him guide us, we can flourish as meat eaters and discontinue with the milk.

Why is this important? **John 10:27** says, *"My sheep hear my voice, and I know them, and they follow me." "And a stranger will they not follow, but will flee from him: for they know not the voice of strangers"* (**John 10:5**).

Not knowing God's voice and following the wind each and everywhere it blows, isn't the best idea. That wind, the wind of confusion, fallacies, and false teaching, can have us end up in a place, following after false prophets, preachers, and teachers, who were never sent by God. What an awful place to end up in!

ONCE SAVED, ALWAYS SAVED

Preach the word; be instant in season, out of season; reprove, rebuke, exhort with all long suffering and doctrine.
2 Timothy 4:2

Apostle Paul, in **Romans 8**, says, *"Who shall separate us from the love of Christ? shall tribulation, or distress, or persecution, or famine, or nakedness, or peril, or sword?* (**verse 35**). *For I am persuaded, that neither death, nor life, nor angels, nor principalities, nor powers, nor things present, nor things to come, Nor height, nor depth, nor any other creature, shall be able to separate us from the love of God, which is in Christ Jesus our Lord"* (**verses 38-39**).

We can come to know Christ in the pardon of our sins, repent, ask forgiveness and walk in our salvation. We want to eternally be with the Father in Heaven. Can we actually do, say, and go wherever we want? The answer is, yes, you can, but that is not a good idea.

When you accept salvation, God puts His Spirit and nature within you. The Bible is clear about not grieving the Holy Spirit, "whereby ye are sealed unto the day of redemption" (**Ephesians 4:30**). In **Psalm 51**, King David, the author, is clearly pleading with God. He said, *"Cast me not away from thy presence; and take not thy holy spirit from me."*

Why would David say that? Why would he ask that? In **John 14:15**, "the Lord said, *If ye love me, keep my commandments."* So, yes, you are saved by the confession of your mouth and heart at that time, but are you continuing to bear fruit? No, not when you are willfully sinning and disobedient. Is that showing the Lord that you love Him?

Let's not just be saved in name only, but through the circumcision of our heart and the inspection of our lives. Let us not take the Lord for granted. Being saved doesn't absolve us as our responsibility to for what God has commanded. Nor, does it mean we won't face the consequences of our actions. God keeps His word, let us keep ours. If we say we are saved, then we must walk in a way that demonstrates that we are and that we spend time with Lord. **Galatians 5:22-23** says, *"The fruit of the Spirit is love, joy, peace, longsuffering, gentleness, goodness, faith, Meekness, temperance: against such there is no law."* Remember, "Not every one that saith unto me, Lord, Lord, shall enter into the kingdom of heaven; but he that doeth the will of my Father which is in heaven" (**Matthew 7:21**). *"And even as they did not like to retain God in their knowledge, God gave them over to a reprobate mind, to do those things which are not convenient"* (**Romans 1:28**).

"But, I'm gifted, so that means I must still be in the will of God (although my life is clearly showing the opposite)." **Romans 11:29** says, *"For the gifts and calling of God are without repentance."* That means you can be operating in them, but there is no power from on high.

In summation, we are the one who determines if we want to be saved and walk in the glory of salvation for a season or a lifetime. God doesn't walk away, but we can certainly walk away from Him. He gives us free will, but it isn't a good idea to use that for evil. **Galatians 5:13-14** says, *"For, brethren, ye* *have been called unto liberty; only use not liberty for an occasion to the flesh, but by love serve one another. For all the law is fulfilled in one word, even in this; Thou shalt love thy neighbour as thyself."*

The problem with the "Once Saved, Always Saved" doctrine is that it gives the illusion that God answers to us. That He lets us do whatever we want and say whatever we want and that we can just stamp His name on us. That's truly a sign of unfaithfulness.

SANCTIFICATION

1 Corinthians 1:30: But of him are ye in Christ Jesus, who of God is made unto us wisdom, and righteousness, and sanctification, and redemption.

Philippians 2:12: Wherefore, my beloved, as ye have always obeyed, not as in my presence only, but now much more in my *absence, work out your own salvation with fear.*

Galatians 5:24: And they that are Christ's have crucified the flesh with the affections and lusts.

Leviticus 11:44: For I am the *LORD your God*: ye shall therefore sanctify yourselves, and ye shall be *holy*; for I am *holy*: neither shall ye defile.

1 Corinthians 5:6: Your glorying is not good. Know ye not that a little leaven leaveneth the whole lump?

Romans 12:1-2: I beseech you therefore, brethren, by the mercies of God, that ye present your bodies a living sacrifice, holy, acceptable unto God, which is your reasonable service. And be not conformed to this world: but be ye transformed by the renewing of your mind, that ye may prove what is that good, and acceptable, and perfect, will of God.

THE ASCENDED

In **John 3:13**, Jesus is talking to Nicodemus. He stated, "And no man hath ascended up to heaven, but he that came down from heaven, even the Son of man which is in heaven." This verse is exactly what people who want to paint the Bible as a fairytale or full of inaccuracies and contradictions would bring up to make a point. The sad thing is, I'm sure many of them haven't done what is instructed for them to do in **James 1:5** (believers included). "If any of you lack wisdom, let him ask of God, that giveth to all men liberally, and upbraideth not; and it shall be given him."

Now, for the record, let me state what verses they would use to contradict what Jesus said in **John 3:13**. First, they would say Prophet Elijah in **2 Kings 2:11** didn't die, but "went up a whirlwind into heaven." Second, they would say Enoch in **Genesis 5:24** (who was a faithful, obedient servant of God) also went to heaven without dying.

However, what Jesus is talking about is His first-hand authority and knowledge of Heaven. Although Elijah and Enoch went to Glory, neither of them were qualified like the One who came back to earth to testify of the goodness of God, to teach, preach, and share the Gospel to the world. They didn't descend back to earth, only Jesus did (the Risen Savior).

Nicodemus knew that Jesus was sent from God, as indicated in **John 3:2**. He said, *"Rabbi, we know that thou art a teacher come from God: for no man can do these miracles that thou doest, except God be with him."*

The truth is, we don't know why God took them to heaven. The Bible didn't specifically say why He chose to do so. Many have speculated that they will be the two witnesses in the end times. However, the Lord didn't reveal why and that will be speculation unless he gave prophetic words confirming that account.

Remember, **Psalm 18:30** says, "As for God, his way is perfect: the word of the LORD is tried: he is a buckler to all those that trust in him." **Isaiah 55:8-9** further states, "For my thoughts are not your thoughts, neither are your ways my ways, saith the Lord. For as the heavens are higher than the earth, so are my ways higher than your ways, and my thoughts than your thoughts."

I think the biggest problem that many have with God is that they cannot control Him. He is God all by himself. He doesn't need our permission to be God. He can heal you without your permission. He can cleanse you, heal you, remove your emotional baggage, sanctify you, and make you whole again—without your permission. Isn't that awesome?

SCRIPTURES ON HEAVEN

Revelation 21:1-4

John 14:2-4

Matthew 6:19-21

Deuteronomy 10:14

Matthew 10:7

Psalm 119:89

Acts 11:19

Luke 23:42-43

Matthew 5:3

Matthew 5:10

HEBREWS 6:1-6

Therefore leaving the principles of the doctrine of Christ, let us go on unto perfection; not laying again the foundation of repentance from dead works, and of faith toward God,
Of the doctrine of baptisms, and of laying on of hands, and of resurrection of the dead, and of eternal judgment.
And this will we do, if God permit.
For it is impossible for those who were once enlightened, and have tasted of the heavenly gift, and were made partakers of the Holy Ghost,
And have tasted the good word of God, and the powers of the world to come,
If they shall fall away, to renew them again unto repentance; seeing they crucify to themselves the Son of God afresh, and put him to an open shame.

WHAT SAY YE?

John the Baptist: *"And saying, Repent ye: for the kingdom of heaven is at hand"* (**Matthew 3:2**).

Jesus: *"Repent: For the kingdom of heaven is at hand"* (**Matthew 4:17**).

Jesus: "The time is fulfilled, and the kingdom of God is at hand: repent ye, and believe the gospel" (**Mark 1:15**).

Jesus: "I tell you, Nay: but, except ye repent, ye shall all likewise perish" (**Luke 13:3, 5**).

Peter: *"Repent, and be baptized every one of you in the name of Jesus Christ for the remission of sins, and ye shall receive the gift of the Holy Ghost"* (**Acts 2:38**).

Peter: *"Repent ye therefore, and be converted, that your sins may be blotted out, when the times of refreshing shall come from the presence of the Lord"* (**Acts 3:19**).

Jesus: *"But go ye and learn what that meaneth, I will have mercy, and not sacrifice: for I am not come to call the righteous, but sinners to repentance."* (**Matthew 9:13**).

SCRIPTURES ON REPENTANCE

Acts 8:22

Acts 17:30

Acts 26:20

Revelation 2:5

Revelation 2:16

Revelation 2:21-22

Revelation 3:3

Revelation 3:19

Hebrews 6:1-6

REPENTANCE

The Lord is not slack concerning his promise, as some men count slackness; but is longsuffering to us-ward, not willing that any should perish, but that all should come to repentance.
2 Peter 3:9

Isaiah 59:2 says, "But your iniquities have separated between you and your God, and your sins have hid his face from you, that he will not hear." This verse is powerful because it shows us that sinning is a matter of life and death. To be separated from God, feels like death. **Hebrews 6:4-6** says, "For it is impossible for those who were once enlightened, and have tasted of the heavenly gift, and were made partakers of the Holy Ghost, and have tasted the good word of God, and the powers of the world to come, if they shall fall away, to renew them again unto repentance; seeing they crucify themselves the Son of God afresh, and put him to an open shame." Those people are what we would call backsliders. **Jeremiah 3:22** says, "Return, ye backsliding children, and I will heal your backslidings."

God puts a profound sense of conviction in your heart for those who are His. It shouldn't be easy to sin and not feel the conviction of Christ when you walk with Him. What becomes dangerous is if there is no conviction at all. Then, one would begin to question if you had the Holy Spirit at all. When a statement like this is made, the first defense is, "You can't judge me." **Matthew 7:16-20** says, "Ye shall know them by their fruits. Do men gather grapes of thorns, or figs of thistles? Even so every good tree bringeth forth evil fruit. A good tree cannot bring forth evil fruit, neither can a corrupt tree bring forth good fruit. Every tree that bringeth not forth good fruit is hewn down, and cast into the fire. Wherefore by their fruits ye shall know them."

To the backsliders, come back and make repenting a daily habit. Repentance is simply admitting that you have gone astray and/or your life is not lining up with the Word of God. God wants all of us to turn back to Him. The Holy Spirit (Comforter) will give nudges, pointing us in the right direction. **1 Thessalonians 5:19-25** says, "Quench not the Spirit." When we follow, we will feel peace. When we don't, there won't be true peace to a true believer. Now, one can pretend they have peace, but that doesn't make it so. That's much like when we know we are called to apologize, and we don't. We go on pretending that everything is fine, but that queasy feeling in our spirits (or stomachs) won't go away until we have done so.

When we repent, we must have an earnest desire to do better, not just mouth the words. We must want to be free from our sins. That's why we ask for forgiveness. We have to die to ourselves. That means we must desire the will of the Father more than our own. His desires will become our desires, and He promised to give us the desires of our heart, if we delight ourselves in Him, trust Him, and commit our ways unto Him. He promises to bring those desires to pass (**Psalm 37:4-5**).

Sin is likened to disease. It can create a deterioration of our destiny and purpose as it slowly eats at our being, robbing us of the joy and peace of the Lord. However, repentance gives

God's permission to continue to help us. We want to eliminate our lustful desires. No, it doesn't always happen overnight for everyone. Everybody's walk and struggles are different. We must make a change in our thoughts, words, and deeds.

For those who solely base your heavenly status on your works, please don't rest comfortably in that. Works can't get you into Heaven. I honestly believe that there will be nothing worse in life than on judgement day if we hear the Lord say, "I never knew you: depart from me, ye that work iniquity" (**Matthew 7:23**). **Matthew 7:21** specifically says, *"Not every one that saith unto me, Lord, Lord, shall enter into the kingdom of heaven; but he that doeth the will of my Father which is in heaven."* In other words, works can't get you into heaven, but not working "out your own salvation with fear and trembling" can (**Philippians 2:12**). The point is one should be careful equating the health of their relationship with Christ based on works alone. It is important to help the Kingdom of God, but we can't be so caught up and preoccupied with busyness (like Martha did in **Luke 10:40**). We can't become so distracted and forget to nurture, fellowship, and foster our relationship with the Lord.

As disciples of Christ, we must strive to be like Jesus. Jesus lived a sinless life, but He died for all of our sins. We are not perfect, but He is perfecting us. Jesus is atoning sacrifice; *"the propitiation for our sins: and not for ours only, but also for the sins of the whole world"* (**1 John 2:2**). Let's stop taking Him for granted. He is awesome. Let's be accountable, loveable, faithful, obedient, submitted, servants of the Most High God.

PEACE BE UNTO YOU

Be free from sin.
Feel the fresh wind of peace upon your spirit.
Fly like the wind.
Soar above the guilt.
Purge your heart, actions, thoughts, and deeds
Whom the son sets free
Is free indeed.
Turn from our wicked ways;
Instability.
A double minded man is unstable.
Repent.
Be forgiven.
Share the Good News.

Do not lay up yourselves treasures on earth, where moth and rust destroy and where thieves break in and steal, but lay up for yourselves treasures in heaven, where neither moth nor rust destroys and where thieves do not break in and steal. For where your treasure is, there your heart will be also.

Matthew 6:19-21

NO OTHER GOD

Ye are my witnesses, saith the Lord, and my servant whom I
have chosen: that ye may know and believe me, and
understand that I am he: before me there was no God
formed, neither shall there be after me.
Isaiah 43:10

I, even I, am the Lord; and beside me there is no savior.
Isaiah 43:11

I have declared, and have saved, and I have shewed, when
there was no strange god among you: therefore ye are my
witnesses, saith the Lord, that I am God.
Isaiah 43:12

THANKSGIVING

Psalm 30:11-12

Psalm 92:1

Psalm 100:1-5

Psalm 107:1

Psalm 136:1

Psalm 150:6

1 Thessalonians 5:18

2 Thessalonians 2:13

Colossians 3:17

Philippians 4:6

Ephesians 5:20

1 Chronicles 29:13

Hebrews 13:15

SCRIPTURES ON COMPASSION

Lamentations 3:22-23

Ephesians 4:32

Zechariah 10:6

1 Peter 3:8

Romans 12:15

Zechariah 7:9-10

Colossians 3:12

Isaiah 54:10

Hebrews 4:15

TO THE DEAF AND BLIND

Bring forth the blind people that have eyes, and the deaf that
have ears.
Isaiah 43:8

God can use any of us. He just needs an obedient, willing
vessel. We can have fully functioning senses, seeing 20/20
and hearing the smallest decibel level of sound, and yet be
blind and deaf in the spirit, to the ways of God, Word of
God, principles of God, thus unable to hear His voice or see
His plan for our life.

Any relationship you want to last takes work. Why do we
work so hard on these natural relationships with others that
are temporary, but neglect the one with the Father that is
long-lasting and eternal? We definitely have to get our
priorities in order.

SCRIPTURES FOR THE DEAF AND BLIND

Exodus 4:10-12

Isaiah 25:5

Leviticus 19:14

Isaiah 42:18

Isaiah 42:19

Isaiah 42:20

Psalms 146:8

Mark 7:32-35

SPIRITUAL NOURISHMENT

Repent ye therefore, and be converted, that your sins may be blotted out,
when the times of refreshing shall come from the presence of the Lord.
Acts 3:19

The joy of the Lord is our strength (**Nehemiah 8:10**). As long as we have breath in our bodies, to sustain our spirit, we must seek ways to daily seek after the Father, renew our minds, and nourish our souls.

Like we establish natural habits and routines in our lives, let us do so in our spiritual lives as well. Sometimes we need to take time away like the Lord did, separating ourselves from others, devoting time to seek the Lord.

There are many things that happen in our lives that we don't understand and sometimes we think the trial(s) will never end. Trust the Master! Incorporate prayer and fasting into your spiritual diets to help you get through those tough times.

God has given us everything pertaining to "life and godliness" (**2 Peter 1:3**). Reading and meditating on scriptures day and night (**Joshua 1:8**) is a great way to replenish your soul, motivate you to keep going, and serve as a reminder that Jesus paid it all for us on the Cross.

THE THREE R'S

Refill

Acts 4:31: And when they had prayed, the place was shaken where they were assembled together; and they were all filled with the Holy Ghost, and they spake the word of God with boldness.

Acts 13:52: And the disciples were filled with joy, and with the Holy Ghost.

Ephesians 5:18: And be not drunk with wine, wherein is excess; but be filled with the Spirit.

Refresh

Psalm 23:3: He restoreth my soul: he leadeth me in the paths of righteousness for his name's sake.

Isaiah 28:12: To whom he said, This is the rest wherewith ye may cause the weary to rest; and this is the refreshing: yet they would not hear.

Jeremiah 31:25: For I have satiated the weary soul, and I have replenished every sorrowful soul.

Repeat

Proverbs 17:9: He that covereth a transgression seeketh love; but he that repeateth a matter separateth very friends.

2 Corinthians 11:16: But though I be rude in speech, yet not in knowledge; but we have been thoroughly made manifest among you in all things.

Philippians 4:4: Rejoice in the Lord always: and again I say, Rejoice.

Acts 3:19: Repent ye therefore, and be converted, that your sins may be blotted out, when the times of refreshing shall come from the presence of the Lord.

THE BIBLE IS...

My daily newspaper,
Television program,
Movie set,
Source of help,
Relief,
Faith,
My everything.
It's trustworthy
It strengthens my salvation.
The words within are
the source of my strength
in which God speaks to me.
It meets my personal needs,
My hope.
It provides me with a pathway to Glory,
A road to heaven,
Instructions for this life,
Promises of eternal life,
Helps me see the light of glory of the Father,
The Son,
The Holy Spirit.

READING THE WORD

All scripture is given by inspiration of God, and is profitable for doctrine, for reproof, for correction, for instruction in righteousness.
2 Timothy 3:16

I accepted Jesus Christ at age of 11 on August 1965. I asked for a Bible for a Christmas present at age 14. I still have it! I realized that reading the Word daily, no matter how many verses, will help us navigate this life. We have to arm ourselves with the sword, which is the Word of God. Although the battle belongs to the Lord, He has enlisted us as soldiers to not only deliver the Good News, but to live accordingly.

It is important that we take time daily to read and dissect the Word of God to get a better understanding. No matter how many times we read the Bible, I am sure we get new revelation every time. Exegeting the text is one of the methods I use that can help me better to understand the scriptures—"precept upon precept; line upon line" (**Isaiah 28:10**).

Exegeting Biblical Texts

AN INTERPRETATION OF CHRIST
JOHN 1:1-18

John 1:1
Word – Jesus

John 1:2
Same – Jesus

John 1:3
Him – Jesus

John 1:4
Him – Jesus
Life – Jesus
Light – Jesus

John 1:5
Light – Jesus
It – (Light) – Jesus
Comprehended It Not – (Did not understand)

John 1:6
There – Here – This - That
Man – John
Sent – brought

John 1:7
Same – Jesus
Came – Brought – Sent
Bear Witness – Tell about, tell of, or speak concerning
Light – Jesus
All Men - World
Him – Jesus

John 1:8
He – John
Not That Light – Not John
Was Sent – Came
Bear Witness – Tell about
That – Jesus
Light – Jesus

John 1:9
That – Jesus
True Light - Jesus
Which – Who – That – Jesus
Every Man – Person – Everyone – Everybody – World
World – People – Every man, every person, everyone, or everybody

John 1:10
He – Jesus
World – People – Every man, every person, everyone, or everybody
Was Made – Created – Form – Invent – Mold – Fixed - Reared
By – Through or from
Him – Jesus
And – But
Knew Not – Did not recognize – Did not see – Did not realize
Him – Jesus

John 1:11
He – Jesus
His Own – People – World – Every man, every person, everyone, or everybody

Received Him Not – Not accepted, rejected, or refused
Him – Jesus
Not – Refused, rejected, denied, or won't

John 1:12
But – However - Anyway
As – While – Duration – While an opportunity – A chance
Many – A Lot – Much – Thousand
Received – Accepted – Be Saved – Repented – Obtained - Welcomed
Him – Jesus
Them – Own People – People – World
Gave - Permitted
He – Jesus
Power – Authority
Become – Accept
Sons – Children
Of – Through, by, or from
God – Father
Even - Although
His – Jesus
Name – Jesus

John 1:13
Which – That – Who – People – World – Everyone – Everybody – Any – Who
Were – Became
Born – At birth
Blood – Flesh – People – Human race – World
Nor – Neither
Of – From – Through – From – By
Will – Blood – People – Human race – World – Man – Every Person
The – These – Those
Flesh – Blood – People – Human Race – World
Nor – Neither
Man – Will – Blood – Flesh – Human race – People – World – Every Person
But – However
God – Father

John 1:14
And – Then
The – This – That
Word – Jesus
Was Made - Became
Flesh – Jesus – Word
Dwelt – Entered – Joined – Walked – Lived – Abode
Us – Children of God – Sons of God
And – Then
We – Children of God – Sons of God – Family of God
Beheld – Saw – Witnessed – Being aware of
His – Jesus Christ
Glory – God – Brightness – Marvelous – Amazement – Wondrous – Light - Shining
Glory – Jesus Christ
As – While

Of – From – Through
The – This – That
Only – Along – With
Begotten – Born – Offspring – Beget - Borne
Of – From – Through – From – By
The – This – That
Father – God – The Word – Christ - Lord
Full – Complete – Fulfillment center
Grace – Jesus Christ – The Word
And – Also – Too – As well as – Even
Truth – Jesus Christ – The Word

John 1:15
Him – Jesus
He - Jesus
Whom – Jesus
I – John (John the Baptist; Forerunner of Christ)
That – Who – Which - Jesus
Me – John (John the Baptist; Forerunner of Christ)
For – Because - Therefore
Was – Existed

John 1:16
And – Because
Of – Under – Through – With - In
His – God
Fulness – Jesus – Christ – Completeness
All – Children of God – Sons of God – Family of God – People of God
We – Children of God – Sons of God – Family of God – People of God
Received – Accepted – Obtained
And - Then
Grace – Jesus – Christ – The Word

For – Upon

John 1:17
For – Because – Even – From – Through – By
The – This – That – Thee – A
Law – Moses – Mandate – Rule – Obey – Management
Was Given – Granted – Accepted – Ruled – Explained – Understood
By – Through – From – Under
But – However – Although – Anyway - Nevertheless
Grace – Jesus – Christ – The Word
And – Among - Plus
Truth – God – Jesus Christ
Came – Sent – Brought – Belonged
Jesus Christ – God – The Word

John 1:18
No – Not
No Man – Nobody – No one – No human person – No human being
Hath Seen – Ever saw – Never saw
God – The Father – The Word
At – From
Any Time – Not at any time – Nowhere – No place – Never seen before ever
The – Thee – This – That
Only – One and alone – One and only
Begotten - Born – Offspring – Beget - Borne
Son – Jesus – Christ – Messiah – Master – Lord
Which – Who – This – That – Jesus – Begotten Son
The – Thy – Thee – This – That
Bosom – Heart – Chest
Of – From – To – Toward – Under – Through
Father – God – The Word – Christ - Lord

He – Father – God – The Word – Christ - Lord
Him – Jesus – Christ – The Light

AT THE REVELATION OF JESUS CHRIST

1 Peter 1:1-25

1 Peter 1:1
Peter
Apostle of Christ

1 Peter 1:2
Foreknowledge of God
Sanctification of the Spirit
Obedience
Sprinkling the Blood of Jesus Christ

1 Peter 1:3
Abundant Mercy
Lively Hope
Resurrection of Jesus Christ

1 Peter 1:4
Incorruptible inheritance
Undefiled
Reserved in Heaven

1 Peter 1:5
Kept by the power
Faith unto salvation
Revealed

1 Peter 1:6
Greatly rejoice
For a season

Heaviness due to temptations

1 Peter 1:7
Praise
Honor
Glory

1 Peter 1:8
Rejoice
Joy unspeakable
Full of glory

1 Peter 1:9
Your faith
Your salvation
Your soul

1 Peter 1:10
Prophets enquired
Searched diligently
Prophesied of grace

1 Peter 1:11
The Spirit of Christ
The suffering of Christ
Christ's Glory

1 Peter 1:12
Preached the Gospel
The Holy Ghost sent down from Heaven
The Angels desire to look into

1 Peter 1:13

Gird up the lions of your mind
Be sober
Hope to the end for the grace

1 Peter 1:14
Obedience
Change mindset and ways
Separate from former lusts

1 Peter 1:15
He that has called you is holy
Be ye holy
In all manner of conversation

1 Peter 1:16
It is written
Be ye holy
For God is holy

1 Peter 1:17
If you call on the Father (Jesus Christ)
Without Respect of Person
Sojourn here in fear

1 Peter 1:18
You know that you were not redeemed with corruptible things
From your vain conversation (foolish ways)
By tradition from your (natural) fathers

1 Peter 1:19
With the precious Blood of Christ

As a lamb without blemish
Without spot

1 Peter 1:20
Christ was foreordained
Before the foundation of the world
Christ was manifest (revealed) in these last times for you

1 Peter 1:21
Believe in God
Raised Jesus from the dead
Faith and hope in God

1 Peter 1:22
Obedience leads to purification
Unfeigned (genuine, sincere) love
Love one another

1 Peter 1:23
Being born again
Not of corruptible seed
By the Word of God (Christ)

1 Peter 1:24
All flesh is as grass
The Glory of Man as the flower of grass
The Grass and flower fall away (lost souls disappeared, gone, passed away)

1 Peter 1:25
The Word of the Lord (Christ) endure forever
The Gospel is preached to the sinners and to the children of God

At age 20, I once preached at a hearing church during a revival. The SPIRIT came upon me, and I spoke what I heard, "Although you can see and hear, you are deaf and blind spiritually, because you refuse to hear and do the Word of GOD.

ABOUT THE AUTHOR

Dr. John H. Manigo was born November 1953 to the late Bishop T.O. Manigo and Evangelist Vivian H. Manigo. John was a faithful husband of 35 years to his late wife, Patricia, and is an incredible father to his son, John Christopher (JJ).

John pastored a deaf church called "Introduce Jesus Deaf Ministries" from 1987-1996 and continues to serve as an evangelist.

John is a graduate of the South Carolina School for the Deaf and the Blind in Spartanburg, South Carolina. He is also a graduate of Tennessee Temple University in Chattanooga, Tennessee, where he majored in Bible Theology. (He sang in the deaf chorus in both institutions). In addition, he received an Honorary Doctor of Divinity degree from the University of Southern Indiana in New Albany, Indiana.

Dr. Manigo has served on numerous boards. In the early and mid-seventies, he was elected Vice President of the Christian Endeavor Society for the Deaf and Chaplain of the Christian Silent Deaf Club.

He received several awards honoring his hard work, dedication, and commitment. He received an award from the Trident Club of the Deaf, and Man of the Year from South Carolina's Black Alumni. John was pictured in *Jet Magazine* in 1976 because he received an award for the Most Outstanding

Deaf Student during his second year at Tennessee Temple University.

Dr. Manigo's hobbies are studying the Bible, reading books about historical events and spiritual doctrines, writing, traveling for ministry, and doing yard work.

His favorite scriptures are **1 Corinthians 6:19-20** and **Philippians 4:13**. He admires the work of Dr. Andrew Foster, Frederick Douglas, W.E.B. DuBois, Martin Luther King, Jr., Mary Bethune, and Sojonurner Truth.

Dr. John H. Manigo authored *Blessed Are the Poor in Spirit* (Volumes 1 and 2) and typed his wife's book *Pray for You and Me* (Patricia C. Manigo). You can find his books online at Barnes and Noble and Amazon.